Hon

J.P.W. Bould

Honesty © 2023 J.P.W. Bould

All rights reserved.

No part of this publication may be reproduced, stored in a retrieval system, or transmitted, in any form or by any means, electronic, mechanical, photocopying, recording or otherwise, without the prior written permission of the presenters.

J.P.W. Bould asserts the moral right to be identified as author of this work.

Presentation by *BookLeaf Publishing*

Web: www.bookleafpub.com

E-mail: info@bookleafpub.com

ISBN: 9789357441698

First edition 2023

For Colin Cooper

ACKNOWLEDGEMENT

It feels fitting that I should first thank Grace Hackett, who was so often a poem's first reader and who's early comments have proved invaluable at every juncture.

To Kacie Deacon who's support and willingness to tell me if I'd written (or done) something stupid can never be shown enough appreciation.

To Olanie Swain for being there when times were toughest.

To Josh Allen for his support when I was writing this collection.

Thank you to those who have provided me with so many Wetherspoons' puddings, film nights, game nights, nights out and bookshop trips: Katie Dackombe, Jenny Gibson, Joey Mayley, Natalie Sharples and Joseph Yildiz.

To Mrs Greswolde, Mrs Lloyd and Miss Roberts for inspiring my passion for English, writing and creativity that persists to this day.

And finally thank you to Colin Cooper and Lorraine Bould who never had the opportunity to read these words.

Memory

I still remember,
The tales of Doncaster Market, the Catering Corps and College;
The pride I hold in my heritage.

I still remember,
The playing of the Beatles, Mahler and Chuck Berry;
The 'Back to the Future' DVD I still own.

I still remember,
The making of cakes, schnitzels and curries;
The not-so-secret trips to McDonald's.

I still remember so much,
The chemical-clean stench of that room,
The one side bloated, the other frail,
The rushed goodbye that I didn't realise would be our last.

I remember it all,
But I remember that the most.

Rain

The punch of the sewing machine,
The splash of a swimming pool,

Half forgotten laughter
Over Easter riddles

All of it's gone now.
All that's left is the silence
Now the Rain has fallen

Haunted Days

I walk between veils and masks
Hearing doors slam and people cry
Endless tears of broken promises.

I'm feeling it too,
In my aching wrists
And spinning stomach
But I keep my mask on,
Even when I want to throw it off,
It's for them I guess.

We're all so fucking broken
And I don't know what to write

Ghost Roomate

You left,
a flight in the night,
no time to say goodbye
and yet you remain
in serial killer's smiles
and pasta covered cupboards,
you haunt us still.

I hope you are happy now
with the damage you wrought,
your parting gift;
an insecure past,
an uncertain future,
a poltergeist at night.

Envy

I stand,
Not alone,
But still isolated.
They have succeeded,
I have not
And I resent them for it.
Conditions met,
They celebrate victory,
I allow myself to cry.
In a moment I am robbed of my future,
As they receive theirs,
Gifts from Oxford and York.
Brighton proclaims endlessly,
Chester seems fuelled by joy,
Bristol offers her false comforts.
I am annoyed by them all,
So I cry some more,
An orphan of the present,
Standing alone,
Isolated in space.

G3, Llandinam

I wasn't supposed to be here,
Something went wrong along the way.

Drunk on my tears
I changed maternity for creativity,
Dales for sea views,
Scrubs for literature.

It goes over in my mind constantly,
Where I should be,
What I should be doing

And the block kills me,
An absence of thought
Serving as quiet punishment
For my ignorance to fate

And all I can hear is:
I don't know what to write
I don't know what to write
I don't know what to write

Do I even belong here?

Call the Poet

I will miss the uniform
(though it was never mine),
it's baby blue comfort
marking my importance.

I will miss the patients
(though I never cared for them),
my only priority
on 12 hour shifts.

I will miss the ward
(though I have never been),
the landing ground
for humanity's miracles.

I don't miss the remarks
(though they are ongoing)
noting the sudden change
of my greatest shame.

Mullion Cove

What did he think,
when he was called to the rage,
deployed with his little fleet
of orange and blue, to search,
to recover the body of the lost boy?

How did he feel,
as the barrage hit his boat,
spraying the crew with sickly salt
from the great waves overhead?
They couldn't wait for calm seas, not with the
lost boy.

When did he know?
That the body he'd rescued,
recovered from the dark depths,
taken home for burial…
When did he first know it was his son?

Who sits with him?
The old lifeboat captain,
resting on the harbour wall,
staring out at Cornish seas,
wishing for his boy to come home.

Midlife

The aftershave announces the arrival,
Layers of its sickly sweet stench assault the nostrils
And in the centre of it,
Him.

Silver-grey gelled back excessively,
A permanent half-sneer,
Beer belly and barrel chest,
Orange and ink coated skin.

Women are 'Loves'
Men are 'Mates',
A mocking laugh,
Every joke finished with a snigger.

Wallet photo of a half-remembered son,
A band of white flesh in place of a ring,
Still argues with 'that Bitch',
Her replacement half his age.

Dickhead.

Sunday Rush

Load the shot,
Brace for the barrage,
The brilliant bullshit,
Sprayed forth by the public.

A click of a button
The filter releases its bounty,
The golden ichor
They so desperately crave.

The milk begins to hiss,
Bubbling to life,
Covered by a glistening potential,
Waiting to be poured

Orders fire from all sides,
Load, click, hiss,
Latte, Cappuccino, Mocha,
Over and over,
All because they're too lazy
To make their own bloody coffee.

Aberystwyth Communist

We all see him coming:
The Aberystwyth Communist

We know to duck and hide
Or be trapped eternally
By conspiracies,
Russian 'victories'
And his favourite 'screamers'
As he chokes us on cigar smoke.

Listen to him now,
Share his knowledge of ghetto,
Learned in Lancashire
Or his AIDS expertise,
Taught by MTV

The Aberystwyth Communist:
Glory in Ignorance

Dear Sebastian

"Dear Sebastian,"
That's how the inscription starts,
A gift from "Xmas '84",
Forgotten in an Oxfam,
Purchased on a whim.
The memories of two strangers,
Held in my unfamiliar hands.

Last Night

I wake up slowly,
Last Night's arms wrapped around me.
Our chests touching,
He watches over me,
With those sea green eyes,
He kisses me
And wishes me a good morning.
We lie there,
Quiet in each others company for half an hour,
Before an infants cry calls him to action.
I stare as he walks away.

I wake up quickly,
Last Night is still asleep,
Her dark hair splayed out,
Obscuring the pillow below,
I pick up her glasses,
From where they lie with mine,
She takes them and kisses me.
She's running late,
I laugh as she rushes to dress,
She goes to the door,
I stare as she walks away.

I wake up alone,

In my bed for two,
Lying foetal in its centre,
Cold and aching.
I force on my glasses,
And reach blindly for the phone,
I stare at the time.
I've overslept again,
Staying up too late,
Writing something mediocre,
Wishing for Last Night.

Grand Central

Moving in stubborn ignorance,
each against the tide,
some at a glacial pace,
others already late.

A vague hubbub
mixes with distorted pop
and a distant child's cry,
a human cacophony.

The overbearing heat
permeates into everything,
making the crowding
all the worse.

New Street Station, 9th September 2022

Monster

The salty squeak of halloumi,
The fat chew of streaky bacon,
The subtle crunch of soft lettuce,
All contained in a moaning bite.

Still it lingers, one hour later,
Blessing the palate
With memories of its presence.

I see now where you get your name,
Oh Monster, giant of your kind.

Thing, a self-portrait

I look into the mirror,
It stares back,
the Thing I despise.

Nails broken by anxiety,
jagged against an itch.

Black-brown forests
protruding awkwardly from the scalp

Glasses lie unbalanced,
falling on uneven ears.

Stretched canyons break,
marking the keratosis stained surface.

Plateaued knees
paired with over-wide feet.

Bloated fat hills roll,
sheened by sweaty rain.

I despite It
and I think,
It despises me too.

Identity Crisis

I am not an urban poet,
I cannot write of sprawling spires
And the untold thousands
Lost to the wild tides of modernity.

I am not a pastoral poet,
I will not write of rolling hills
And the forgotten few
Trapped in the rhythms of antiquity.

L Plate

A pitying smile,
As he clips growing wings.

A gentle sigh,
'I think you know you failed'.

What Creativity Will Do

It's amazing,
what creativity will do,

When it's starved,
fed only with lies
used to placate the concerned.

When it's assessed,
a grade assigning worth,
to an individual truth.

When it's forgotten,
left unused by its owner
save for an uninspired 500.

When it's quoting,
another recital of Ritchie's lines
in the shaving mirror.

When it's trapped,
forced into a future,
it hadn't planned.

It's amazing,
what creativity will do
as it destroys itself.

Blunt Edge

A glint of silver
shining under harsh light,
cool steel, a blunt edge
running across soft skin,
setting off the neurones
and sending shivers down the spine.

How would it slit?
How would it slice?
How would it slash?
Staining with crimson
the marks of misadventure.

Far better, I think,
to stick with a blunt edge.

Angel

You stand there now,
on its edge,
the great rock precipice,
wind blowing at your face.

You could be free now,
take a leap of faith.
After all this,
maybe you'll fly.

Milton Keynes UK
Ingram Content Group UK Ltd.
UKHW020145220823
427215UK00016B/982